THE PASSION
– THROUGH THE EYES OF OTHERS –

The Passion

through the eyes of others

JAMES TRAYNOR

Illustrations by Peter Edwards

McCrimmons
Great Wakering, Essex, England

First published in United Kingdom in 2005 by
MCCRIMMON PUBLISHING CO LTD
10-12 High Street, Great Wakering, Essex SS3 0EQ
Telephone 01702–218956   Fax 01702–216082
Email: info@mccrimmons.com
Website: www.mccrimmons.com

Illustrations
© PETER EDWARDS

Narrative text
JAMES TRAYNOR

ISBN 0 85597 663 2

Design and layout by Tania Dauptain and Nick Snode
Typeset in 11.5/14pt Clearface Regular and 24pt Aesop
Printed on 115gsm coated art
Printed and bound by Thanet Press Ltd., Margate, Kent   A/0E

Contents

- 1 -

Jesus is condemned to death

PILATE'S STORY

He troubled me. He was too quiet, too silent – and it seemed to me that in that silence lay his strength. I've ordered many people to their deaths. You have to if you want to keep order. My paymasters expect me to keep a tight lid on things – these Jews are a troublesome lot. But this man was different. He was definitely a Jew – but he was unlike any of the others. Usually when you sentence someone they start kicking and screaming, pleading, begging. But he was different. He troubled me. He was strangely peaceful. It was as if he could see beyond me – and beyond the events that were unfolding. He, not I, was in control of his life. I had the power to sentence him to death but he wasn't frightened or intimidated by me. He spoke of truth and witnessing to the truth. Such talk left me feeling uneasy and once he spoke this way I was anxious to be rid of him. I sentenced him – but the questions remain. At night when I'm waiting for the sleep that never comes – I see his face and hear him speaking. *'I came into the world for this – to bear witness to the truth and all who are on the side of truth listen to my voice.'* He stops me from sleeping and how I crave for the peace he had. How I would love to have his silent strength.

PRAYER

> *Lord, Jesus Christ,*
> *Give us the courage:*
>> *to be silent in your presence;*
>> *to rid our hearts and minds of the*
>>> *meaningless chatter that stops us from*
>>> *drawing closer to you;*
>> *to have the courage to uphold the truth of your*
>>> *Gospel in all things and before all people.*

- 2 -

Jesus takes up his Cross

ZACCHAEUS' STORY

Once I'd been sitting in a tree looking down at him. He was popular then and surrounded by fawning crowds. Today he was surrounded by a crowd all right, but they weren't fawning now – this time they were baying for his blood. I remember that tree – it was a sycamore, good and sturdy, and it gave me a vantage point, helped me to see him. He looked up at me and from that first eye contact my life was transformed. Now here was another tree for me to remember. They had quickly made a cross and the wood was rough and crude. You could see that rough edges were digging into his shoulders. The crowd were impatient to see his death and the cross was pressed onto his back. He took it willingly and freely. On the day that I had climbed the sycamore tree I was anxious to see what kind of man Jesus was. Today I saw exactly what kind he was. He looked at me again. There was still nothing but love and acceptance in those eyes – and there was something else – strength and power. It was as if he really did believe that he was bearing this humiliation on behalf of everyone. I know what it's like to be hated and he was being hated now. In my time, I've planned all sorts of revenge and dreamed of pay-back time. There was none of that with Jesus. The really scary thing is that he never stopped loving – me, the soldiers, the crowd, everyone. He just kept on loving.

PRAYER

Lord, Jesus Christ,
Give us the courage:
 to love our enemies and
  pray for those who persecute us;
 to accept whatever cross we are asked to carry
  in life;
 to follow you in your patience and acceptance.

- 3 -

Jesus falls for the first time

THE RICH YOUNG MAN'S STORY

I once ran after him. I saw him in the distance and I needed to speak to him. By the time I caught up with him, I was
exhausted and I fell at his feet, hot, sweaty and covered in
dust and grime. He reached down to me on that day.
My riches didn't impress him nor was he bothered about
my appearance. He helped me up and looked me in the eye.
He told me there was one thing I lacked… But you know

the story anyway. Everyone spoke about it for weeks after-
wards. They spoke of the rich young man – as if I didn't
have a name… But I digress. On that fateful day I saw **him**
fall. This time it was he who was covered in dust and grime
and… – blood. Oh the blood – it was everywhere. There
wasn't any of his garment that wasn't splattered or stained.
He fell. For a moment, it looked as if he wasn't going to get
up. People started spitting at him, the soldiers kicked and
the crowd goaded and jeered. Then someone shouted 'God
have mercy on you.' He looked around to see who it was
but there were too many faces. But whoever it was, it
seemed to give him strength. It was as if God himself was
reaching down to him. He heaved himself to his feet, stead-
ied himself and walked on. He didn't look back. That day I
knew. I knew like I had never known before…

PRAYER

Lord, Jesus Christ,
 Your cross was heavy – and you fell.
 You struggled on
 You climbed back to your feet
 You drew strength from the love of your Father.
Remove the pride
 that prevents us from asking for help.
Remove the hardness of heart
 that prevents us from praying for those in need.

– 4 –

Jesus meets his mother

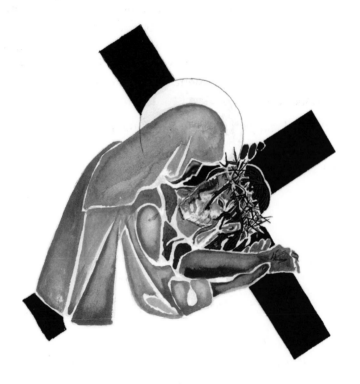

THE WIDOW OF NAIN'S STORY

I looked at her. I saw her pain. I knew what she was going through. I too had lost a son, my only son.

She stood there. There's hardly a mother in the world that can stand by and watch a child of theirs suffer without wanting to swap places. You could see in her face that she was no different. She shook with grief. Their eyes met and it was like the exchange of a million words in half a second.

They did not need to speak. Their relationship was like so many other relationships between mother and son; a knowing glance, a loving smile, a nod of acceptance. She reached out to touch him but was forced back by the soldiers. But she was strong and beyond intimidation. She forced her way through the crowd, following him every step of the way, and several times their eyes met and each time you could see that they were drawing strength from each other. They spoke silently and it was as if she now understood fully and for the first time.

Eventually I caught up with her and touched her arm. She turned and looked at me and looked back at him and then I began to understand too…

PRAYER

Lord, Jesus Christ,
  In the meeting between you and your mother
    you united yourself with all who suffer in
    silence.
  Help us to realise that
    we can never fully know the pain of another.
  Help us to respect all who suffer and
    to be ready to walk alongside them –
    sometimes in silence – but always in
    mutual respect and support.

- 5 -

Simon helps Jesus to carry his Cross

SIMON'S STORY

I didn't have any choice. When you come from an oppressed minority group you don't have many rights. At first, I was resentful. What did all this have to do with me? I didn't even know the bloody and battered figure as he struggled under the weight of the cross. The crowd wanted their blood sport and it was important that he was still alive to face the planned execution. The first thing that struck me was that he was interested in me as a person. The Romans had just grabbed me from the crowd – a big, fit looking individual – someone up to the task in hand.

They weren't interested in anything other than that. But he was. He turned and looked at me, squinting through the blood and sweat that was running into his eyes. "What is your name, my friend?" "Simon", I replied. "Thank you, Simon", he said. We never spoke again. I didn't have the energy for small talk – that cross was heavy – but we didn't need to talk. A bond had been forged. He had called me by name and from his battered state had conferred on me a dignity that I did not deserve and which melted my earlier resentment at being forced into an argument that wasn't of my making or of my choice.

Late that afternoon, I did find out his name. I went back to Calvary and read the inscription above his head. *Jesus of Nazareth, King of the Jews*. Some said that he didn't look like a king. I thought very differently, but then I had heard his voice speaking through the pain and the blood and the torment, and I had seen his strength.

PRAYER

    Lord, Jesus Christ
      Simon helped you –
        even though at first he was unwilling to get involved.
      Help us to be willing to become involved
        wherever you continue to suffer;
      Help us to be willing to help
        wherever people are oppressed or exploited;
      Help us to be willing to be counted.

Veronica wipes the face of Jesus

VERONICA'S STORY

People say that I am a woman of ill repute. I was a companion of Mary Magdalene before her conversion. We worked together. We had little or no choice. Once you get a reputation, no one wants to know you and if you've children to feed you sometimes go to desperate lengths. Mary Magdalene often urged me to go and speak with him but I was too scared – and I was stuck in a rut. No one likes living the way I do – but I needed the money.

He passed by, no more than an arm's length away. He looked a complete mess. There was a big man helping him to carry the cross but it looked to me like he would die before ever he reached the top of the hill. Someone tried to offer a cup of water but was forced back by the soldiers. I saw my chance. I ran forward and used my shawl to wipe his face. We looked at each other – two wretches looking into each other's souls. In that instant I knew I was free – I felt as Mary Magdalene had felt. I burst into tears but they weren't tears of sadness. They were the tears of liberation and freedom. Both of us had nothing to offer except ourselves and in that moment God touched my heart in a way that no one had ever touched me before. There was no need for words. I didn't want a sermon and I had nothing to give except my wretchedness. I gave him brief respite from the pain and discomfort – he gave me back my dignity and my soul.

PRAYER

Lord, Jesus Christ
  In showing yourself to Veronica
    you revealed yourself as
    the God of love,
    the God of forgiveness and
    the God of compassion.
  Help us to reflect that same love,
    forgiveness and compassion
    to those around us
    so that they too may see your face.

Jesus falls the second time

THE SOLDIER'S STORY

Normally I enjoy my work. We're paid well. We have the best food, the pick of the women – and when we're off duty the wine is good and free. Sometimes there's a bit of blood sport too. Pilate is keen on keeping the Jews in check. There are plenty of executions and plenty of beatings. Today was just such a day. Some of the lads were a bit edgy. They'd heard that this Jesus character had claimed to be from God – and that he'd performed miracles. I don't hold with that twaddle. I'm a professional and it was just another execution as far as I was concerned. The crowd were up for it too. The scribes and Pharisees had them whipped up into a frenzy. They were a bloodthirsty crowd, I tell you.

He kept falling and we had to enlist someone to help him. A big bruiser of a guy, but that didn't stop Jesus falling. When he fell the second time I got really angry. I yanked him to his feet and kicked him for good measure. He turned to me and said "Thank you". I smacked him one across the face for being so insolent. He kept on looking at me. I convinced myself he was just catching his breath, drawing strength from the pause in the struggle but those eyes left me feeling uneasy. It was like I was staring into something over which I could never have any real power. I turned away and in that moment I knew myself for what I was – not brave at all but a weakling and a coward.

PRAYER

Lord, Jesus Christ,
Help us to be brave and courageous
when confronted by evil.
May we never resort to bullying of any kind –
verbal or physical.
May we always learn from you
who are gentle and meek in heart.

Jesus comforts
the women of Jerusalem

THE WOMEN'S STORY

We have no names that anyone would recognise – but we have dignity. He gave us that dignity. Before he came we were third-rate citizens. It was a man's world, a man's religion, a man's temple. Women stayed at home and did as they were bid. He wasn't afraid to be seen with women, he mixed with us – made us feel good, told us we were important and valued. Whenever you sat with him you felt as if you were in the presence of someone very special.

The Scribes and Pharisees said he was a fraud – but you never heard a woman say that. There's not one of us that wouldn't have taken the place of Simon the Cyrenian. Each one of us would willingly have helped to carry his cross but there was no way we could get near. So we followed – staying as close as we could. Once when he paused for breath he turned and saw us. He saw our tears. *"Don't cry for me"*, he said – *"Cry rather for yourselves and your children"*. Later we argued about what he meant. We each had our own interpretation. As we grew older and became grand-parents we learned that the killing never stops. The hatred and bloodshed; the prejudice and oppression. They go on and on and on… Do you think, perhaps, that that's what he meant?

PRAYER

Lord, Jesus Christ
  Help us to rid our world of hatred and bloodshed;
    prejudice and oppression.
  Let there be love shared among us,
    let there be peace in our hearts
  and let the search for a just and peaceful world
    begin with us.

- 9 -

Jesus falls the third time

THE STORY OF HANNAH, MOTHER OF JUDAS

There had been a time when Judas was full of excitement and zeal. He wanted me to accompany their party to Jerusalem. He felt that big things were going to happen. He'd given up his job to follow Jesus; he really believed in him, that he was the one who was going to free us from the oppression of the Romans. Gradually he became disillusioned. Then it all turned sour and the speed of events in those last few days was overwhelming. I was staying at an inn and a friend came to tell me that Judas was dead – he'd hung himself from a tree and, apparently Jesus was to blame. I went rushing to find Jesus and there he was crumpled on the floor beneath a heavy cross. My mind was in a whirl – what was going on. There seemed to be chaos everywhere. Jeering, chanting crowds, blood and sweat and an atmosphere of complete anarchy. It was as if we had all gone to sleep and awoken in hell.

I looked at Jesus. As he lay there in a heap, all our dreams seemed to have crumpled with him. I called out his name. He turned and looked at me. He must have sensed my grief, my complete lack of understanding – but he didn't turn away. It was as if he was willing me to trust, to keep on believing. But how could I? When you're overwhelmed with grief how can you keep focussed on some bigger picture that you cannot understand? He struggled to his feet. The blows rained down on him and the jeering and spitting took on renewed frenzy. He looked for me again in the crowd. He looked hard at me and somehow, I don't know where from, I was given an inner strength. Why did I suddenly find the ability to trust? I don't know. But crazy and mad though it seems now, I did trust – and I followed him to Calvary – in my pain and my grief and my anger. And I cried and I sobbed and I broke my heart – but I followed him.

PRAYER

> *Lord, Jesus Christ*
>> *Sometimes it's not easy to follow you.*
>> *Sometimes we have more questions than answers*
>>> *and many times the attraction of giving up*
>>> *is very appealing.*
>> *Help us to imitate you;*
>>> *to keep on picking ourselves up,*
>>> *to keep on persevering to the end –*
>>> *no matter how hard the journey becomes.*

– 10 –

Jesus is stripped of his garments

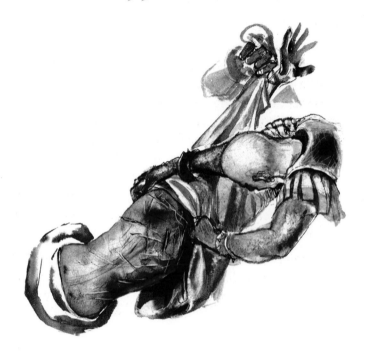

BALTHAZAR'S STORY

I was back in Jerusalem for the festival. I had spent many years travelling, completing my research and the time for writing up my studies meant that I needed a base. Jerusalem seemed as good a place as any. I'm old now but I remember the first visit there – and the journey on to Bethlehem where we found him, as clear as if it were yesterday. He was born in abject poverty. We had followed a star; we knew something important was happening. People spoke of God having visited his people. We three had an open mind and we went in search of answers. We found the young girl with her husband and their baby. She was just bathing him and he sat in the bathtub – a baby like any other, loving the water, gurgling and splashing and beaming at his audience.

But that was years ago. Now, back in Jerusalem I saw him again. This time a fully-grown man, stripped naked in front of a hostile and jeering crowd. At first it was hard to believe that this was God visiting his people. But though the abject poverty was still there, there was a peace about him. It was as if he knew that this was the fulfilment of all that God had planned for him. Bloody, beaten and battered he was nevertheless a man of faith and strength and character. He remained someone of immense dignity. There was no anger in him – no spite, not a hint of vengefulness – and this was where his strength lay.

I was mesmerised by him. Years ago I had followed that star, transfixed by its brightness and promise of something wonderful. I looked at him now and saw a similar promise.

PRAYER

Lord Jesus Christ,
    You willingly accepted humiliation and pain.
    In them lay the foretaste of the glory
        that awaited you in the Resurrection.
    Help us to remain focussed on your promise
        that we will all share in eternal life
        if we but follow your way.

Jesus is nailed to the Cross

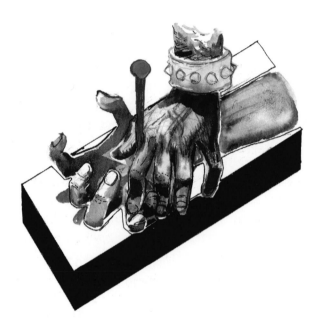

JETHRO'S STORY – THE DEAF MAN

He had once healed me of my deafness. For the first time in my life I heard the life-giving sound of laughter, the birds singing, the noise of water rushing over stones, the recitation of prayers in the Temple and the joy of conversation. I heard all these things because he once whispered into my ear "Ephphatha". He had truly blessed and transformed my life.

I stood now praying that I could once again be deaf. The jeering and insults from the crowd were an obscene and hideous sound. But there was worse to come. The sound of tearing flesh as the nails were driven into the rough wood of the cross was too much to bear and I held my hands over my ears trying to shut out the noise. Please God, let me be deaf once more!

Eventually the banging stopped and they lifted the cross so that his weight pulled down on his hands, tearing once more at the flesh. Every now and then he would try to find comfort from the tugging and tearing, try to catch a breath; you could see the pain etched on his face. He didn't cry out or shout aloud but he said something that silenced everyone watching. *Father, forgive them…* To me it was the most powerful thing I've ever heard. I'm used to silence – I lived many years in total silence – but the silence of the crowd after he'd uttered those words was like the silence of self-condemnation. You know what I mean – that awful and awesome eerie silence that haunts us when we're faced with the consequence of some sinful action or selfish word. It's a silence that's laced with self-recrimination. I'd heard one of his sermons when he had preached the need to forgive enemies and pray for persecutors. On that day, he practiced what he preached.

PRAYER

> *Lord, Jesus Christ,*
> > *You prayed for your persecutors and*
> > > *begged forgiveness for those who*
> > > *had wronged you.*
> > *Give us courage to imitate you.*
> > *Help us to be generous in heart*
> > *That the world may be transformed*
> > > *through your suffering.*

Jesus dies on the Cross

JOHN'S STORY

I stood there with Mary, His mother. It was eerily calm. There'd been an eclipse and the world had gone dark for several hours. It was almost as if God were venting his anger. If I'd had any doubts up to this stage, they were gone now. Some of the other disciples had run off – nervous, scared, frightened – even confused. They didn't understand how it could have ended this way. I was lucky because I'd never doubted that he was in God's hands. His last words to Mary and me were that we should each look after the other – and then he turned his prayer to his Father: *Father, into your hands I commend my spirit...*

The crowds had long since gone and now it was raining – not heavy rain – just a refreshing shower, almost as if the clouds were anxious to gently wash his body, cleansing it of the grime and blood. The ground around us soaked up the water and, like his life, it was gone. A soldier came. He had orders to deliver one final wound and with his spear he sliced into Jesus' side releasing a flow of blood and water. It was over. All had been accomplished.

PRAYER

Lord, Jesus Christ,
   Your weakness is stronger than human strength
      and your folly is wiser than human wisdom.
   In the cross is your victory.
   In the cross you began the transformation from
      death to life.
   Give us the courage to rise above
      all that the world sees as important
   Give us the courage to willingly embrace
      all that you ask of us.

Jesus is taken down from the cross

JOSEPH OF ARIMATHEA TELLS HIS STORY

I watched the whole thing from afar – I've always been a coward at heart. I could have been braver, been there throughout the trial and suffering. Instead I looked after my own interests and kept quiet. I looked on now. John, his disciple, was there at the foot of the cross along with Mary, the mother of Jesus. They held each other in a bond of mutual respect and love. It was an intensely moving scene and it seemed intrusive to break their silent grief. So I approached, nervously, aware that I had been conspicuous through my absence throughout the events of the last few hours. However, at least I had bought a tomb and had arranged for the return of his body. One of the soldiers managed to prise the nails from the wood and we placed his lifeless form into the arms of Mary his mother. She sat for a while, holding his head, gently rocking back and forth. I imagine she did that many times when he was a small baby. We left her to her own thoughts and prayers.

PRAYER

Lord, Jesus Christ
Your lifeless form was handed back to your
mother and the circle was complete.
She held you in birth and held you in death.
Help us to see that you are Lord of all things,
that everything is unfolding according to
your will.
When all seems dark and empty
help us to trust in you
and in the power of your name.

Jesus is laid in the Tomb

NICODEMUS' STORY

I had first approached him in the dead of night. I was a prominent Pharisee – and I had my reputation to think of – but there was something about him that perplexed and perturbed me. Despite this, whenever I was in his company I felt reassured. He had that ability to make you feel at peace. So I would seek him out whenever I could. We would talk and discuss into the small hours but I could never be absolutely certain that he was the Chosen One, the Messiah we were awaiting. Part of me wanted to believe that he was – but the conservative in me wouldn't let me take that step of faith into the unknown.

Joseph of Arimathea had arranged with Pilate to take the body away for burial. I had in my possession about a hundred pounds of myrrh and aloes mixed together. We wanted to anoint and prepare his body. There was just a handful of us when we laid him in the tomb. His mother was there, John his disciple, a couple of the women, Joseph and me. The crowd had had their fill; their lust for blood had been satisfied and they had all gone home.

I looked at his lifeless body. His mother gently and tenderly applied the ointments and when we had covered him with the cloth we came away. I turned back to look at him for one last time. I was still asking myself 'Was he the Chosen One of God?" I couldn't be sure but there had been something about the way he had faced death – he preached forgiveness right to the end and never once cried out in anger against his persecutors. Perhaps he really had been the Messiah we'd waited so long for and what had we done to him…

The first time I had approached him had been under cover of darkness; as I came away from that tomb it was getting dark once more.

PRAYER

Lord Jesus Christ
By your own three days in the tomb
you made holy the graves
of all who believe in you
and by so doing, strengthened the hope of
resurrection in those whose bodies are subject
to decay.
Remove all doubt from our minds
that we might truly believe
that you are the chosen one of God.

- 15 -

The Resurrection

MARY OF MAGDALA TELLS HER STORY

I felt such an idiot. I had gone to the tomb with more spices and ointments. I wanted to do something. I felt so helpless and the grief was making me feel hopeless. The tomb was empty. I saw this man in the garden where the tomb was. I thought he was the gardener and when I couldn't find the body I asked him if he had moved it. He turned and looked at me and said, quite simply "Mary". He always called people by their names, always was a great respecter of individuality. He called me by my name – and looked at me and in that instant I knew. I saw with full knowledge. It was as if a huge mist had cleared and I saw everything clearly and as if for the first time. "Go and tell the brothers…" Did he really think I could have kept quiet? Everything he had said about his rising from the dead was true. Impossible though it seemed it had happened. I was filled with an inner peace, a serenity, a sense of calm. Not even the emotions I'd experienced when I'd wept over his feet and dried away those tears with my hair could compare with my feelings now. He had conquered death – and death no longer held sway over us.

I ran as fast as I could to find the others. When I found them all I could do was blurt out: "He is alive – He is risen as he said he would." And then I cried – but not tears of sadness. They were tears of gladness and joy and relief and happiness and fulfilment. He is alive! Alleluia, Alleluia!!

PRAYER

> *Lord, Jesus Christ*
> > *You conquered death and*
> > > *invite each of us to share in your victory.*
> > *Help us to closely follow where you have gone*
> > > *that victory may be ours*